Fashion Painting Step-By-Step

TABLE OF CONTENTS

Applicator Paints

Dimensional Paint

Use TULIP dimensional paints right from the applicator bottles to create fashionable, dimensional designs. Dimensional paints can also be applied by brush to paint iron-on designs or to fill in large areas. Apply dimensional paints with sponges to make wonderful hand printed fabrics. Exciting abstract designs can be achieved with paint spreaders and pallet knives. Use cardboard strips to create sweeping lines or fancy blended streaks. Rhinestones, beads and other embellishments can be set directly in beads of wet paint for easy application to garments.

TULIP dimensional paints are available in ½ oz., 1 oz. 4 oz., and 8 oz. applicator bottles. Choose from four different finishes: Slick Paint, dries bright and shiny, Iridescent Paint, colors give a pearl-like luster, Glitter Paints for sparkling, glittery designs, and Puffy Paint results in a soft, dimensional matte finish.

All TULIP dimensional paints are available in a wonderful assortment of fashion colors.

For lites out fun, paint a design with TULIP Glow in the Dark, and Neon Nite Lites. Dimensional paints that glow in a variety of colors.

Tulip Dyes

TULIP fabric dyes can be used in several different ways to achieve a variety of fashion looks. Squeeze dyes straight from the applicator bottles to damp or dry fabrics for line art designs. Mix dye with water (60% dye-40% water) in a plastic spray bottle and spray garments to cover large areas with a pretty mist of color. Simulate the tie dye look using rubber bands. TULIP Dyes do not require heat setting, simply air dry for 24 hours. Launder before wearing garment to restore shape and to soften fabric.

Candi Crystals

Add sparkle and glitter to painted designs with Candi Crystals. Simply, snip the tip for easy application right from the tube! Hold the paint tube right on your shirt and squeeze gently. Move your hand slowly as you make squiggles, lines, dots and shapes. Artist style paint brushes work great to fill in large designs. Use paint spreaders, plastic spoons or cardboard strips to spread Candi Crystals into exciting abstract shapes. Combine 2 or more colors to make rainbow designs. Choose from an assortment of brilliant colors available in 2 oz. or 4 oz. applicator bottles.

Spatter Paint

Create bright abstract designs in seconds with Spatter Paint. They are fun and easy to use right from the applicator pump bottle! Create spatters, streaks and splotches. Simply hold spray bottle about 6″ from your garment and spray on spatters. Move your hand while pumping the paint to make exciting spatter streaks! To make big, bold splotches, hold the bottle close to your shirt and pump in one spot. Combine all 3 techniques for a funky design. Try the same techniques with Spatter Mania (not shown). It's similar to Spatter Paint but without the pump. To use, simply squeeze or shake the applicator bottle for instant spatter designs!

Brush-on Paints

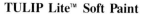

TULIP Brush-on paints are fun and easy to use right from the jar! Try them all! Why not combine them for a variety of vibrant colors and interesting textures?

TULIP Lite™ Soft Paint

Soft Paint is the perfect match for TULIP Transfers! The shaded transfers turn ordinary garments into a detailed canvas ready for painting. Tulip Soft Paints allow details of transfer to show through for perfect results everytime and Soft Paint colors feel as soft as your shirt! Available in 24 blendable colors, Soft Paint works great for any fashion design on white fabric.

Fashion Tints

Add a glimmering look to all your designs with lusturous Fashion Tints. These sparkling brush-on shades work well with shaded transfers, too! Brush the soft colors on clothing to create a subtle shimmer. Colors blend easily for beautiful shaded designs.

Liquid Glitter

Add a glitzy look to all your fashions with TULIP Liquid Glitter. Brush, layer, spread or stencil onto clothing for a rich, smooth, glittering appearance. Choose from a variety of vibrant colors. For added sparkle, set rhinestones and "gems" into wet Liquid Glitter Paint.

Fiber Fun™

Brush on to create the ultimate in eye-catching glitz and sparkle. Fiber Fun contains metallic fibers that create an entirely new texture. Choose from beautiful colors in a tinted or clear base. For a different look, spread, stencil or sponge onto your designs.

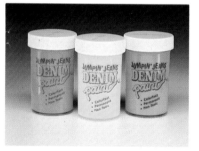

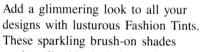

Jumpin Jeans™ Denim Paint

Opaque and brilliant on denim, and all dark fabric, Jumpin Jeans Paints are available in Brites, Glitters, Neons and Metallics. Available in sizzling colors that cover dark fabrics completely in one application. Use it directly from the bottle with a brush. Create wonderful designs by stenciling or sponging. Denim paint also works great for highlighting and outlining. Remember, it's not just for denim!

Designer Metallics

Add a smooth, glimmering sheen to your designs with TULIP Designer Metallic Paint. Brush it on right from the jar for super one coat coverage, even on dark fabrics. Blend 2 or more colors together to create new shades. Stencil, and outline with Designer Metallics, too!

Fashion Suede™

Create the look and feel of soft suede with TULIP Fashion Suede Paint. Transform an ordinary painted surface into a luxurious suede finish with a few seconds of steam from your home iron. The elegant shades add a fashionable look to denim, sweatshirts, accessories and more!

3

Week End Wear

CREATIVE EXERCISE
Edie Yerardi, designer

Get a running start in this comfortable and fashionable sweatsuit. A perfect start to fashion painting fun. Learn the simple, basic techniques and create outfits to take you through the whole weekend in style!

Materials Used
White cotton or cotton blend sweatsuit
TULIP SLICK PAINT COLORS:
Flourescent Pink
Flourescent Green
Turquoise
Yellow
Raspberry
Lavender
Black

Silver Glitter Paint
TULIP by Marx paint Spreaders
Masking tape

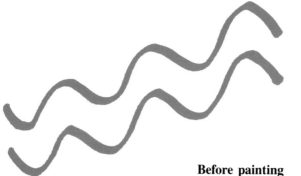

Before painting

Wash and dry new garments. Line sweatshirt with shirtboard, wax paper or plastic.

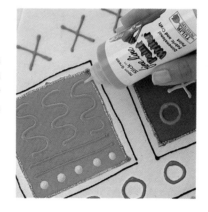

Use masking tape to make eight squares on your sweatshirt.

Squeeze the Slick color of your choice inside first square. Make a puddle of paint about the size of a nickle and spread the paint inside the masking tape using paint spreader or a flat brush. Continue until you have painted the entire square.

Paint inside all remaining squares using the Slick colors.

Let paint dry and remove masking tape.

Practice making squiggles, circles, dots and dashes on a paper towel. Using the photo as your guide, make similar dimensional designs in each of the eight squares.

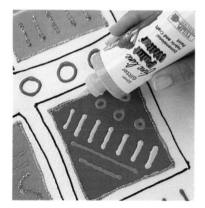

Outline each box with Silver Glitter Paint. Then make a Black Slick line around the squares as shown.

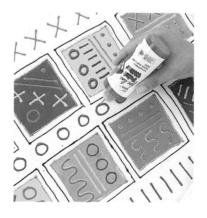

Make rows of XXX's, OOO's and lines above, below and between the rows of squares.

Use these same simple steps to add a few decorative squares to your matching sweatpants.

Week End Wear

THREE LEAVES
Edie Yerardi, designer

It's always fun to have a pretty new Tee shirt for the weekend. This leaf design can be painted in any number of color combinations to co-ordinate with your wardrobe. The sponge painted designs are so fast and easy to do; you'll have this technique mastered in no time at all!

Materials Used
Leaf Green Slick Paint
Turquoise Slick Paint
Navy Slick Paint
Liquid Pearl Iridescent Paint
3 kitchen sponges
Paper or plastic plates

Before painting
Wash and dry new shirt and line with shirtboard, wax paper or plastic.

Trace the three leaf shapes on tracing paper. Cut out the shapes and place on sponges. Draw the leaf patterns on the sponges. Cut the sponges to shape.

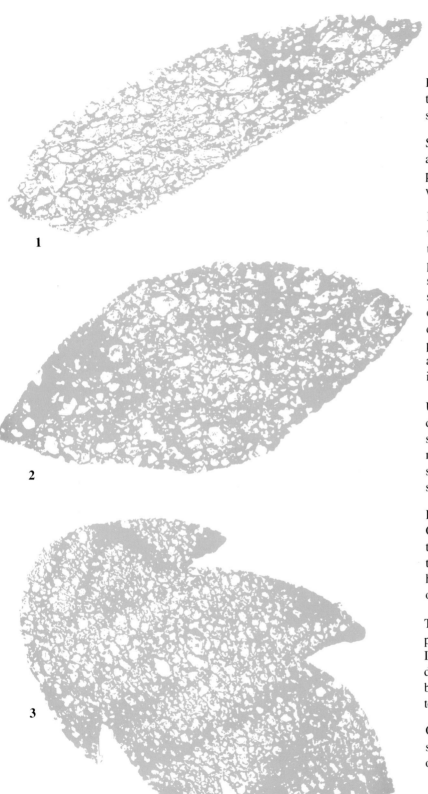

1

2

3

Rinse out all three sponges, squeeze out the water and pat dry. Sponges should be slightly damp while painting.

Squeeze a puddle of Turquoise Slick Paint about the size of a half dollar on paper plate. Spread the paint around on plate with plastic spoon or cardboard.

Press the thin leaf shape sponge down on wet paint. Turn it over and check to see if the entire sponge has been coated with paint. You will want the texture of the sponge to show. You may want to practice sponge painting or check your design first on a paper towel. Simply press sponge down on paper to print design. You can print more than one design before re-applying paint to sponge. This will create interesting shades and textures.

Using the first leaf shape sponge, paint the design from shoulder to waist of shirt as shown. You can always go back and add more of this design so start first with several leaf prints scattered down your shirt.

Repeat this printing process using the Leaf Green and Navy Slick Paints and the other two leaf shapes. One color does not have to be dry before printing a second. Notice how the leaf shapes have overlapped each other and vary in direction and placement.

The final accents to add to your leaf pattern are the beads of Liquid Pearl Iridescent Paint. Practice making dimensional pearl beads on a paper towel by simply holding the applicator tip next to the paper and squeezing gently.

Once you are happy with the size and shape of your practice beads; paint clusters of the pearly white droplets on your shirt.

Week End Wear 3

LOOP DE LOOP
Edie Yerardi, designer

You'll be sure to receive many compliments while wearing this fashion top and you'll have the fun of saying "I made it myself!" Start with a simple black sweatshirt or a cotton jersey top, add dimensional and brush-on paints, set in stones and add a little lace trim. Here's how to do it...

Materials Used

Black cotton jersey top or sweatshirt
TULIP Gold Designer Metallic
Gold Fiber Fun
Turquoise Slick
Turquoise Glitter
Liquid Pearl Iridescent
Liquid Gold Iridescent
Bronze Iridescent
Magenta Gem Iridescent
2 yards flat turquoise lace
2 yards 1″ ruffled white lace
Clear acrylic rhinestones
Chalk pencil
Ruler
Flat brush 1/2″

1. Fold your shirt in half and mark the center point three inches up from knit band. Use a ruler and chalk pencil to draw a big V from the shoulders down to bottom center point. Measure from top (neckband) center equal distances to shoulders. Mark with chalk.

2. Line your shirt with shirtboard before painting.

3. Use a flat brush to paint half circles of Gold Designer Metallic and Gold Fiber Fun. Fill in the big V area with the half circles, changing the positions of the designs as you paint.

4. Set the clear acrylic rhinestones with Turquoise Glitter Paint. Squeeze out a bead of paint about the same size as the stone, then just press the stone down in the wet paint. The paint should surround the stone completely for good adhesion to the fabric. Scatter several rhinestones on your design and set in place.

5. Using the Turquoise Glitter Paint, make zig zag designs. Once you have mastered the simple art of dimensional squiggles on a paper towel, paint the zig zags as shown across your design area.

6. Next, paint the dimensional Turquoise Iridescent wave designs.

7. Now, add the Magenta Gem beads of paint right from the applicator tube.

8. Use Bronze Iridescent paint to make the small half circles and Gold Iridescent to paint the three line motif.

9. Let your shirt dry flat on shirtboard.

10. When the paints are completely dry, add the lace trim. Start with the flat turquoise lace and pin down from shoulder, making a fold at the bottom of V then follow up to the opposite shoulder.

11. Add the white ruffled lace on top of the turquoise. Pin and sew in place.

12. Enjoy wearing your exciting fashion top!

Using these same techniques, why not create a beautiful hair accessory to match your top?!

5 CLASSIC PRINT
Victoria Wells, designer
Create this classic print from the iron-on design and paint with the dimensional paint colors of your choice. Gold and White Iridescent paints were used on the model shirt.

4 ZIG ZAG
Victoria Wells, designer
Playful patterns in several bright Slick colors. So simple to do right from the tube! First paint the White Slick rope design. Make loops in the design and fill in with bright shapes of Slick colors. Paint geometric outlines, circles, triangles, squares, and fill them in with simple little shapes of bright Slick colors.

6 GOLD MEDALLIONS
Victoria Wells, designer
It takes only one color to create this beautiful designer fashion. Simply iron on the motifs and paint with Liquid Gold Iridescent Paint. Set clear acrylic stones with the same paint.

Back To School

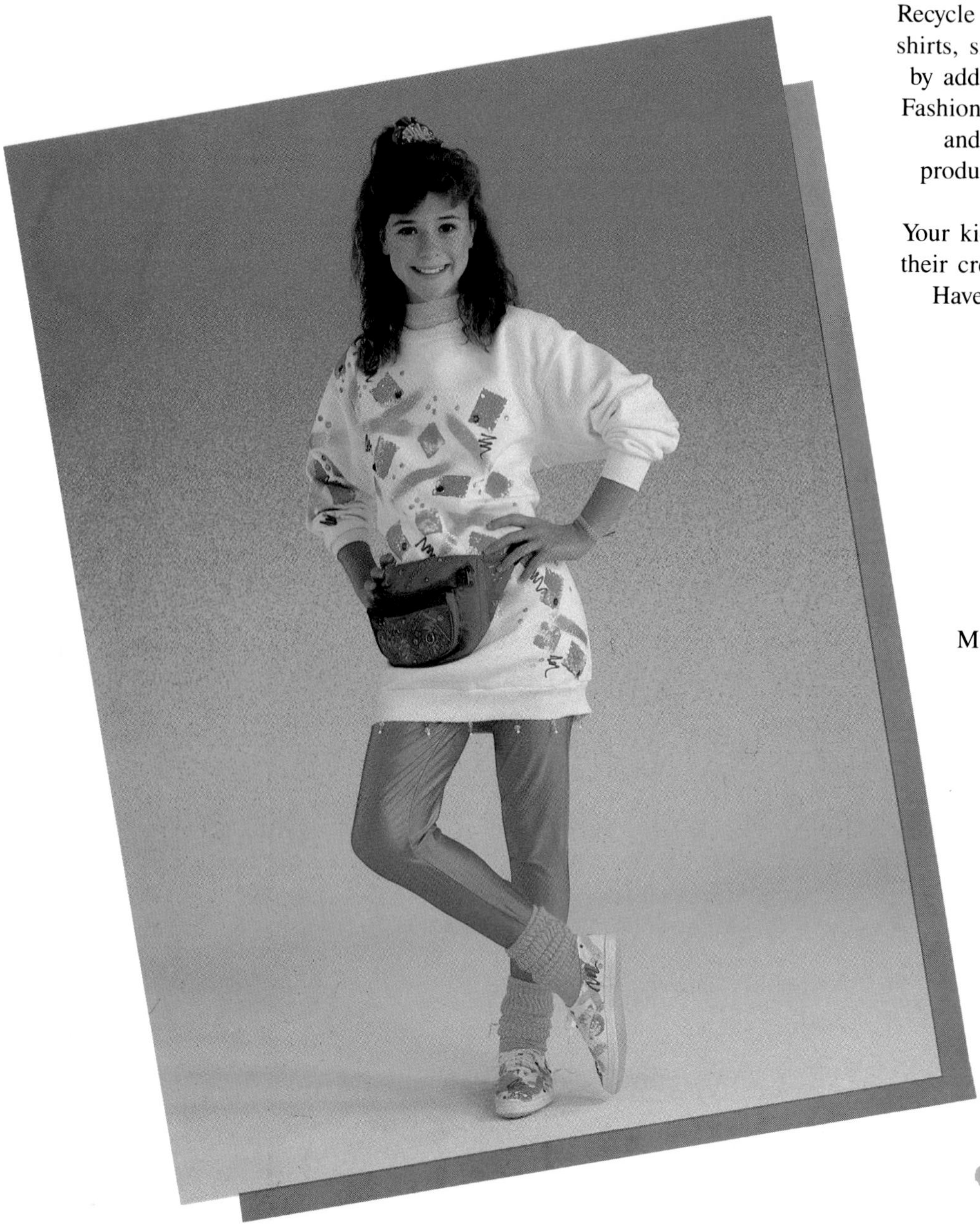

Recycle last seasons sweatshirts, Tee shirts, sneakers, backpacks and caps by adding colorful painted designs. Fashion Painting is great family fun and entertainment. The finished products make wonderful gifts for kids birthday parties, too! Your kids will learn how to express their creativity and individual style. Have fun painting together, it's a great rainy day activity!

Materials Used

White sweatshirt
Raspberry Candi Crystals
Plum Candi Crystals
Blueberry Candi Crystals
Lavender Slick Paint
Baby Blue Slick Paint
Silver Glitter Paint
Magenta Gem Iridescent Paint
Purple rhinestones
Assorted beads for fringe
Needle & thread
Pencil with flat eraser top
Kitchen sponges
Medium flat fan brush
Scissors
Paper or plastic plates
Water bowl

Easy to do sponge painting, squiggles, dots and streaks create lots of fashion fun on this sweatshirt, sneakers and belly bag.

Before painting

Wash and dry new sweatshirt and line with shirtboard or plastic. Remember to line the sleeves, too. Cut two kitchen sponges to size, one square about 2″ × 2″ and one rectangle about 2″ × 3″. It is easiest to cut the sponges while they are slightly damp. You can draw the shape with a permanent marker, then simply cut with scissors.

Painting

First paint the Magenta rectangle shapes. Squeeze a generous amount of Magenta on a paper or plastic plate and spread it around with a brush. Use the rectangle sponge that is just slightly damp, and press it in the wet paint on plate. Check to see if you have an even coat of paint covering the sponge. You may want to practice a few sponge prints on a paper towel before printing on your shirt. Make several Magenta rectangle prints as shown on the body and sleeves of your shirt. Notice that the direction of the sponge changes with each print.

Repeat this process using the Baby Blue Slick Paint and the square sponge.

The next step is to make the sparkling Candi Crystals streaks. This is simple to do, just squeeze out a big bead of the crystal paint and using your fan brush, spread and feather the paint as shown. Use the Plum, Blueberry and Raspberry Candi colors to create the sparkling streaks.

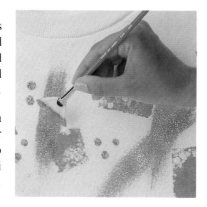

Add to your design by printing Candi dots with a pencil's eraser. Squeeze a little Candi color on a paper plate, dip the end of the eraser in wet paint and press to shirt. Use this technique to add dots of all three Candi colors, scattering here and there on your design.

Now you are ready to make dimensional squiggles of Lavender Slick Paint. Practice your squiggles on a paper towel and when you are happy with your skill, add several squiggles to your design.

Attach the rhinestones to your shirt. Just make beads of Silver Glitter Paint about the same size as the stones. Press the flat back stones into the wet paint. The paint should form a little ring around the stone. Let dry flat overnight.

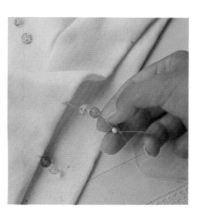

You can make bead fringe and sew to the bottom of your shirt. Measure and mark placement of fringe, then sew the little strings of beads as shown.

Back To School 2

WAY TO GO!
Lee Riggins, designer

Kids love the bright tie dye look! Here's a way to achieve that fashion look without the mess!

Materials Used
Boys' shirt
White Tee Shirt, cotton or cotton blend
TULIP DYE COLORS:
Lime
Orange
Lemon
Aqua
Brite Blue
Black Slick Paint
Plastic spray bottle

Disappearing marker
Plastic bags

High top sneakers and cap
TULIP SPATTER PAINTS:
Fluorescent Green
Fluorescent Orange
Yellow

Backpack
Silver Designer Metallic Paint
Orange Denim Paint
Small round brush
Small flat brush
Chalk pencil
TULIP SLICK COLORS:
Black
Fluorescent Orange
Fluorescent Green
Marigold
Cardboard
Scissors

Before painting

Wash and dry new shirt and line with plastic. Divide shirt into five sections using a ruler and blue disappearing marker. Mark the sections with dots of the color of dye you want in each.

Mist the entire shirt with plastic spray bottle. The shirt should be damp but not dripping wet.

Painting

Make dots of the dye colors directly from the applicator bottle. Using Lemon first, fill in the entire center stripe.

Repeat dots of Orange, Brite Blue, Aqua and Lime dye colors, making the bold stripes as you go. See how the dots run and blend on the damp fabric.

You may need to mist your shirt as you go if the fabric becomes dry. This direct dye method works best on a damp fabric.

After the dye is completely dry, you can iron-on the transfer designs and paint with dimensional Black Slick Paint. Remove plastic liner while ironing.

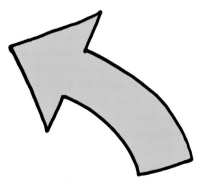

Family Casuals

RAINBOW TROUT
Terry Johnson, designer

This pretty rainbow trout design is as much fun to paint as it is to wear! Use the iron-on design and paint with sparkling tints to create the shaded rainbow.

Materials Used

White cotton or cotton blend Tee shirt (this design would also look great on a white sweatshirt)
TULIP FASHION TINT COLORS:
Sunset Gold
Sno White
Tropical Water
Fern Green
Lilac
Mauve
Red Geranium
Black Slick Paint
Black fine line permanent marker
Medium round brush
Small round brush

Before painting
Wash and dry new garments. Line shirt with shirtboard, wax paper or plastic.

The first step is to iron the rainbow trout design to your shirt. Next, use a fine line permanent black pen to draw over the transfer lines. This will make a darker, more permanent impression.

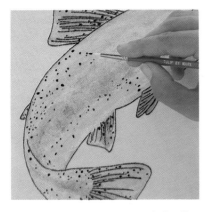

Painting the black dots and details is next. The objective is to paint different sizes and shapes to create a natural look. To do this, squeeze a little Black Slick Paint on a paper plate. Wet your small round brush and mix a drop of water in the paint. Practice making differing dots on a paper towel. Apply varying amounts of pressure to the top of your brush. See how this results in interesting and irregular small dots. When you are happy with your skill, start painting the details on the fish. Dip your brush in the paint after painting three or four dots. Refer to the illustration and paint the details on upper fin, body and tail.

Complete your design by painting the eye as shown. Let dry 24 hours.

Painting

Begin painting by applying Sno White Tint to the body of the fish. Use a medium round brush. You will be painting over this color while it is still wet. Paint the following tint colors (in this order) to create the rainbow: Tropical Water, Fern Green, Red Geranium, Mauve, Tropical Water, and Lilac at the bottom. Overlap and blend the colors as you paint the rainbow. Clean brush in water and blot dry between color changes.

Paint Sunset Gold around the eye and mouth area. Add a touch of Red Geranium and blend the colors with your brush.

Next, coat the fins above and below the body of the fish, with Sno White base. Shade the top fins with Fern Green and Tropical Water. Add a touch of Sunset Gold to the top fin for sparkle.

Paint Lilac around the edges of the lower left fin and use Gold in the center. Use only Gold on the lower fin.

Coat the twisted tail area with Sno White. Paint the colors in the same order as body to continue the rainbow down the tail.

Use Mauve, Fern Green, and Tropical Water to complete painting the end of tail.

Let the tints dry completely before continuing.

Family Casuals 2

DAD'S FISHING VEST
Lael Furgeson, designer

bait

sinkers

bass

Gone fishin'

Cast Off

Catch

trout

hooks SALMON

Dad or grandpa will be the talk of the pond in his whimsical fishing vest. Gather your family together for the decorating fun. It is as much fun to paint as it is to wear! And, who knows...this vest could even attract some fish!

Use an assortment of Slick, Iridescent and Glitter colors to decorate the vest. Draw bright, dimensional designs right from the tube, or, first draw designs with a chalk pencil.

BEARFOOT CAMPER
Cathy Cahill, designer

Here's a fun sweatshirt for anyone in your family to wear. The little eyes peeking out of the tent are painted with Glow-in-the-dark paint for extra lights out fun!

Materials Used
White sweatshirt or Tee shirt
Copper Iridescent Paint
Jade Green Iridescent Paint
Khaki Frost Iridescent Paint
Black Slick
Gun Metal Iridescent Paint
Green/Gold Iridescent Paint
Glow-in-the-dark Paint
Small round brush

Before painting
Wash and dry new garments and line shirt.

Iron on the "Bearfoot Camper" design.

Painting
Use Bronze Iridescent to paint the tree trunks right from the tube. Paint dimensional leaves with Jade Green. Use a small round brush to paint the tent with Khaki Frost. Brush Black Slick Paint to inside of tent. Use the Black Slick right from the tube to paint ropes and outline tent. Paint the rocks with Gun Metal. Paint the green foliage. Paint the bear tracks with Gun Metal. Paint eyes with Glow-in-the-dark. Add the black eyeballs when dry.

Elegant Fashions

POSTCARDS
Victoria Wells, designer

This brightly decorated pink top shows several painting techniques used to create sophisticated fashion designs. You'll be surprised at how simple it is to learn these decorating techniques and create exciting fashions for your wardrobe.

Materials Used

Pink sweatshirt
(cotton or cotton blend)
TULIP LIQUID GLITTER COLORS:
Silver
Gold
Crystal
Royal Blue
Ocean Spray
Dusty Rose
Black Slick Paint
Liquid Pearl Iridescent
Gun Metal Iridescent
1″ sponge brush
White chalk pencil
Black permanent marker

Before painting, wash and dry new garments and line with a shirtboard or plastic.

The first step is to trace the "Postcards" design to white netting using a permanent marker. Piece and tape the pattern together then trace the entire design to the net.

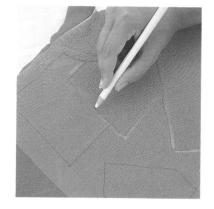

Pin the net design in place on your shirt. Trace all the outlines of shapes to shirt using a chalk pencil. Notice how the chalk goes through the net to fabric. After you complete tracing the front designs, you can trace a few of the geometric shapes to shoulders.

Fill in all the shapes with Liquid Glitter. Using a sponge brush, paint the shapes with the Gold, Silver, Dusty Rose, Crystal, Royal Blue and Ocean Spray Liquid Glitter colors.

Now, you are ready to add the beads of paint that outline all the shapes. Start with the Gun Metal Iridescent and squeeze dimensional beads around the outline of first shape. Remember to start your paint on a paper towel and make a few practice beads before painting on your shirt. Next, outline the second shape with White Liquid Pearl Iridescent. Continue to add the outlines of beads, alternating between the Gun Metal and Liquid Pearl colors.

Let your paints dry before continuing.

Place the net design over your painted design and trace the swirls and decorative designs to the inside of shapes using a black permanent marker.

Next, paint all the White Liquid Pearl patterns right from the applicator bottle.

The last step is to paint the Liquid Gold and Black Slick dimensional accents inside the shapes. Notice the chain of Black Slick dots that connects from shape to shape. You can draw the chain with a chalk pencil before painting to plan the lines.

Let your paints dry flat for 24 hours.

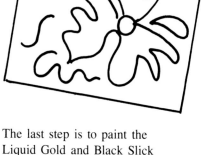

Elegant Fashions 2

POINTS
Victoria Wells, designer

Materials Used
Fashion Tee
(cotton or cotton blend)
TULIP IRIDESCENT
PAINT COLORS:
Bronze
Liquid Pearl
Liquid Gold
Gold Glitter Paint
Black permanent marker
White chalk pencil
White fine tulle net
Paper towels

Dimensional lines and beads of paint make up this simple, yet sophisticated fashion design. Start with a plain black, long, sleeve fashion Tee and transform it into a sensational, designer original! This same design would also be beautiful on a creamy white fabric.

Before painting

Wash and dry new garments and line with shirtboard or plastic.

Transfering design

Piece together the paper pattern sheets and tape together. Place the white bridal tulle net over design sheet and tape to secure. Use a permanent black marker to trace the entire design to net. Remove paper and put the net design on your shirt. Pin in place. This design looks best when extended across one shoulder to mid back. Transfer the design to your shirt by tracing over the lines with a white chalk pencil.

Remove net. Use your net pattern and trace a portion of it over the shoulder and across the back.

Painting

This entire design is made up of dimensional lines and beads of paint. Remember to start your paint flowing on a paper towel before painting your shirt. If you have not as yet painted dimensional beads and lines, practice on a paper towel until you feel comfortable with your skill.

Begin painting the design by first outlining all the "points". Start with Bronze Iridescent and outline the small leaves at neckline. Working your way across and down the design, use the Gold Glitter and Liquid Gold Iridescent to outline as shown. Next use the Liquid Pearl to paint double rows of beads creating outlines for the three "points".

Next fill in the "points" with beads and lines of dimensional paints.

Fill in the Gold Glitter outlines with slightly larger glitter beads.

Make Liquid Gold lines inside the outlines. Paint a center line and then paint connecting lines to meet the outer edge, similar to the veining pattern in a leaf.

Let your design dry and complete the painting of the "points" on the back.

Won't your friends be surprised when you tell them you painted this lovely fashion yourself?

Mother, Daughter Fashions

SUNDRESS DESIGN
Lael Furgeson, designer

Paint these sweet little flowers on a white sundress, T shirt or sweatshirt and surprise your special little girl! Use the iron-on design and pretty shades of pink with turquoise and lavender accents.

Materials Used
White cotton sundress
TULIP Slick Paint colors:
Dusty Rose
Turquoise
Lavender
Green/Gold Iridescent
Neon Pink Candi Crystals
Small round brush

Before painting
Wash, dry and line sundress.

Iron-on design
Place the iron-on design on sundress and center the design to make a yoke pattern. Transfer to dress. Cut and pin additional portions of the design to fill the yoke of the dress you are decorating. Transfer to dress. If the fabric you are decorating is thin, place a sheet of aluminum foil between the front and back of garment to keep the transfer ink from going through to the back. Cut several flowers from design sheet and iron on a cluster to the skirt as shown.

Painting
1. First paint the outlines of each flower. Use Dusty Rose Slick and make dimensional outlines right from the applicator.
2. Next paint the lines that create the pretty plaid design. Use Lavender and Green/Gold Slick colors. Let paints dry before continuing.
3. Use a small round brush to paint the inside of each flower with Neon Pink Candi Crystals.
4. Paint small dimensional beads in the centers of flowers with Liquid Gold.
5. Add the dimensional beads of Turquoise Slick Paint. Let dry flat for several hours.

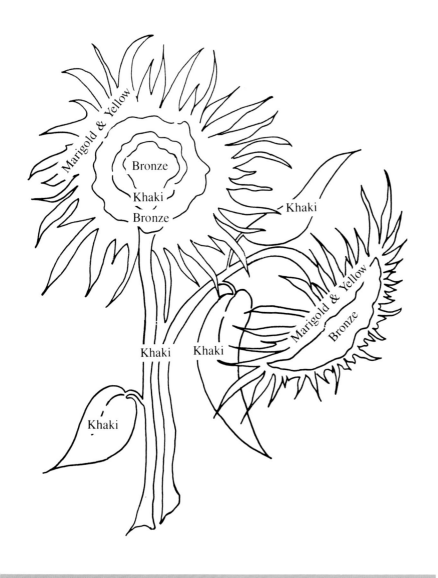

Marigold & Yellow

Bronze

Khaki

Bronze

Khaki

Khaki

Khaki

Marigold & Yellow

Bronze

Khaki

SUNFLOWER SHIRT
Lael Furgeson, designer

Materials Used
White sweatshirt
TULIP Slick Paint Colors:
Marigold
Yellow
TULIP Iridescent Paint Colors:
Khaki Frost
Bronze
Gun Metal
Small round artist's brush

Before painting
Wash and dry new shirt.

Place iron-on design to fabric and pin in place. Press on the "Sunflower" design. Line your shirt with shirt board or plastic.

Start at the top of the design; use the small brush and Marigold Slick Paint to fill in the outer flower petals.

Next, use Yellow Slick and go over a few of the petals so that they are lighter in color.

To fill in center of the largest flower, dab brush into Bronze Iridescent. Leave thick in some areas. With Khaki Iridescent, fill in the specified are in the same manner; leaving paint thick in some places. Mix some Gun Metal with the Bronze in the center of the flower to darken the color. Repeat this step on the other flower, too!

Fill in the stems and leaves with Khaki Frost. Finally, make tiny dots around the neck and cuffs. Make them heavier near the edge, and more sparse as they go down the neck and up the sleeves.

Let design dry overnight.

Neon Pink
Candi Crystals

Liquid Gold

Turquoise

Dusty Rose
Outline

Green/Gold

Lavender

Green/Gold

Lavender

Lavender   Green/Gold

Holiday Fashions

HOLIDAY TOYS
Lael Furgeson, designer

Make this fun holiday sweatshirt for a special kid on your list. It's easy to do with simple sponge painting and iron-on designs!

Materials Used
White sweatshirt
TULIP DENIM PAINT COLORS:
Neon Pink
Neon Orange
Neon Yellow
Neon Green
Neon Blue
Yellow
Green Slick Pen
Silver Glitter Paint
Gold Glitter Paint
Black Slick Paint
Fl. Orange Slick
Chalk pencil
Small round brush
Kitchen sponge cut 2″×2″
Paper plate
Plastic spoon
Paper towels

Before painting

Wash and dry new sweatshirt and line with shirtboard or plastic.

Use a chalk pencil to mark the squares for the checkerboard. This will give you the positions for the iron-on toy designs.

Iron-on the toy designs in between the checker board squares.

Cut an ordinary kitchen sponge into a 2″×2″ square. Rinse sponge and wring out water, blot on towel. Your sponge should be just slightly damp for painting.

Spread a generous amount of Neon Green Denim Paint on a paper plate. (You can also use Neon Green Slick for this step.)

Press your sponge in paint and make a print on a paper towel to be certain the square has an even coat.

Print all the checkerboard squares with the Green Paint.

Paint the toy designs with a small round brush. Use lots of bright colors, as shown. You may want to let the green squares dry before painting toys so you won't accidentally smear the paint.

Add the dimensional accents. Use the Slick Paint and Glitter colors to add the details to the toys and christmas tree.

Paint dimensional outlines around squares with Fl. Orange Slick Paint.

Let your Holiday Toys design dry flat overnight.

Holiday Fashions 2

CANDY CANES
Lael Furgeson, designer

Wouldn't a little girl you know love to wear this sweatshirt for the holidays? You can make this design fit any size shirt, just paint more or less candy canes to fit.

Materials Used
White sweatshirt
Red TULIP Dye
or Red Slick Paint
Lime Green TULIP Dye
or Green Slick Paint
Gold Glitter Paint
Red Ruby Iridescent Paint
2 paper plates
1 kitchen sponge
2 yards of 1/2" plaid ribbon
Small gold safety pins
Scissors
Permanent marker

Before painting

Wash and dry new sweatshirt and line with shirtboard or plastic.

Cut sponge for painting. Cut one small sponge about 1½″ square. Trace the candy cane shape and cut out of paper. Place paper cut out on sponge and trace the candy cane shape with a permanent marker. Cut out the shape.

Sponge paint the red candy canes and green squares as shown. Turn the sponges as you print so the designs have a random, scattered pattern "falling down" the front of the sweatshirt. It's fun to add a few designs to the sleeves, too!

Remember to keep your sponges slightly damp when painting.

It's best to make a few impressions on a paper towel before printing on your shirt. Spread the paints on plastic or paper plates, press sponge to paint and print on a paper towel to check. Sponge painting is so easy to do, it's great for kids, too!

Now, you can add the dimensional beads of Red Ruby Iridescent Paint and the squiggles of Gold Glitter. Practice on a paper towel and when you are happy with your designs add them to your shirt.

As a final fashion accent, add plaid bows to your design. Simply tie several bows and pin to shirt with small safety pins. Remove when laundering.

Use these same supplies to create wonderful holiday gift wrap. Use inexpensive plain paper and sponge print the candy cane designs using these same techniques.

Holiday Fashions

JINGLE BELLS
Lael Furgeson, designer

You'll have fun wearing this pretty and comfortable holiday fashion top and you'll be proud to say "I made it myself!"

Materials Used
Red sweatshirt
Silver Designer Metallic
Gold Designer Metallic
Green Liquid Glitter
Silver/Clear Fiber Fun
Jade Greeen Iridescent
Red Ruby Iridescent
Gold Glitter Paint
35 or 40 1/2″ red acrylic stones
Medium round brush
Small flat brush

Before painting
Wash and dry new sweatshirt.

Place iron-on design to fabric and pin in place. Press on the "Jingle Bells" design. Line your shirt with shirtboard or plastic.

Iron-on pattern in back of book.

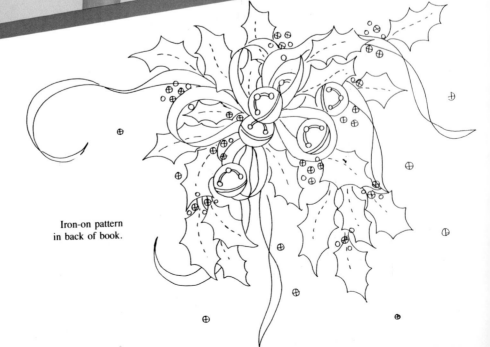

Start painting the gold bells first. Use a small round brush and Gold Designer Metallic Paint.

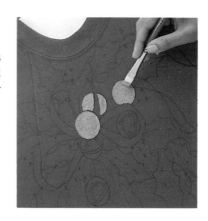

Next, paint the ribbons using Silver Designer Metallic. Once the silver is dry, use the Silver Fiber Fun to add wonderful texture to the ribbon. Simply paint the Fiber Fun over the ribbon using a small flat brush.

Now you are ready to paint the leaves. Use the Green Liquid Glitter Paint to fill in all the leaf shapes.

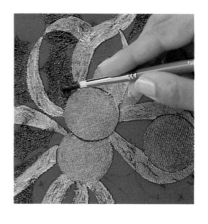

Outline the leaves with dimensional paint right from the applicator bottle. Use the Jade Green Iridescent to outline and add the veins to all leaf designs.

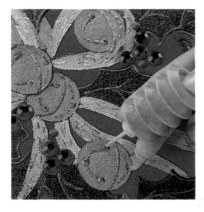

Outline the bells with the Gold Glitter Paint. Paint dimensional lines around all the bells and add the details to the inside.

The final step is to set the rhinestones and add the dimensional "berries" to your design. Use the Red Ruby Iridescent and paint beads of paint about the same size as the rhinestones. Use the small X's on the pattern sheet as a guide for placement. Set stones in the wet paint and press in place. Add additional red "berries" as shown.

Designing With Dyes

STARS & STRIPES
Jan Murdock, designer

TULIP Dyes are easy to use right from the tube or mix with water and spray on fabric like we have done to create this terrific "Stars and Stripes" design.

Materials Used
White Tee shirt
(cotton or cotton blend)
TULIP DYE COLORS:
Raspberry
Teal
TULIP Silver Glitter Paint
Plastic spray bottle
Masking tape
(½″ wide and 1″ wide)
Scissors
Cardboard
Plastic bags
Silver nailheads

Before Dyeing
Wash and dry new Tee shirt and line with shirtboard and plastic to keep dye from running through to back. (Line the sleeves, too.) Protect your work area as well.

Adhere masking tape to shirt to make the four stripes. Use the 1″ tape to make the first stripe and use the ½″ tape to create a second stripe about an inch below. Use a yardstick to help keep your lines straight. Apply the tape from sleeve to sleeve.

Next make the stripes 7″ down on shirt. Use the ½″ tape first then repeat the 1″ stripe an inch below. Cover the section between the four stripes with plastic. Tape plastic over this area to protect it from the Raspberry dye spray.

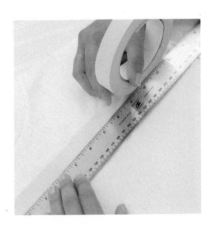

Mix the Raspberry TULIP dye with water in spray bottle. Dilute dye to 60% dye to 40% water ratio. Shake to mix. Spray the dye mixture to top and bottom sections of your shirt. Let dry flat before continuing. Use a hair dryer to speed up drying time.

Remove the protective plastic from center of shirt. Cover the top and bottom areas that are now dyed to protect from the next dye application. Use plastic and tape it down securely. Mix the Teal dye with water using the same 60% to 40% water ratio. Shake to mix. Arrange the star cutouts in the center section of your shirt. Refer to photo for placement. Be sure the stars are laying flat on fabric. You may want to use double face tape to secure.

Spray the star area with the Teal dye mixture. Let dry before continuing.

Remove the star cutouts from shirt and you'll see your star pattern. Remove all tape and plastic.

Outline all the star shapes with Silver Glitter. Simply make dimensional outlines right from the applicator. Let dry before adding nailheads.

Arrange nailhead studs in the Teal area scattering them around the stars. Push the prongs through fabric and bend the prongs with a metal spoon.

*Tip: to seal the prongs of studs, turn shirt inside out and paint a small dot of Silver Glitter over them. Let dry flat.

Shirt can be laundered after 48 hours.

Designing With Dyes 2

STARBURST
Jan Murdock, designer

Create fashion magic from inexpensive Tee shirts and TULIP Dye. This random starburst pattern is simple enough for kids to do. Use the TULIP Dye colors or your choice and these same techniques to make terrific Tee shirts to coordinate with your wardrobe.

Materials Used
White Tee shirt
(cotton or cotton blend)
TULIP DYE COLORS:
Lemon
Fluorescent Green
Aqua
Plastic spray bottle
Rubber bands
Scissors
Plastic bags

Before painting
Wash and dry new shirt and protect your work area with plastic bags.

1. Use rubber bands to make random starbursts on your shirt. Poke up about 2"-3" of fabric and wrap the bundle of fabric tightly with rubber bands. Use both the front and back of shirt together when making the bundles. Wrap the rubber bands in a random fashion around the fabric. This random wrapping is what adds the lines inside the starburst. Repeat this banding as many times as you like over your shirt, don't forget the sleeves.
2. Apply the Lemon dye right from the applicator to the bundles of fabric. Do not try to cover the entire bundles, as you want to leave white streaks in the starburst designs.
3. Sprinkle Lemon dye around outside of bundled up area. Just shake the applicator to create dots with the dye.
4. Turn your shirt over and squeeze Lemon dye from bottle into each of the bundles and sprinkle dots of dye around each .
5. Mix the Fl. Green dye with water (60% to 40% water) in plastic spray bottle. Shake to mix. Spray the scrunched up shirt with the Fl. Green dye. The more you spray the more intense the background color will be. Turn shirt over and spray the reverse side with the Fl. Green.
6. Cut away all the rubber bands, be careful not to cut your shirt. Flatten out your shirt and let dry a couple of hours.
7. Use the Aqua dye to sprinkle dots from the center of the starbursts out, holding the bottle about 12" from your shirt. Move your hand while squeezing dye applicator to add random streaks.

Let shirt dry completely, then wash to soften and straighten out fabric before wearing.

3

ABSTRACT ALL OVER
Jan Murdock, designer

Abstract shapes cut from cardboard are used to create the white background designs around which we painted the shades of blue dye. Add Bronze Iridescent line art and you have a sensational new original outfit!

Materials Used
White cotton Tee shirt and leggings
TULIP DYE COLORS:
Aqua
Brite Blue
Navy
Purple TULIP Spatter Paint
Bronze TULIP Iridescent Paint
1″ trim brush
(available at hardware stores)
Cardboard
Scissors

Before starting
Wash and dry new garments and line with plastic bags.

1. Cut shapes from cardboard similar to those shown. Make them the appropriate size for your garments.
2. Using three mixing cups: Mix Aqua dye with water, 2 parts dye to 1 part water. Mix Brite Blue dye and Navy dye, using the same mix ratio.
3. Arrange your cardboard cutouts and double stick tape them to your garment.
4. Start painting the dye mix colors on your shirt using trim brush. Start at the neckline and work down the front making intersecting shapes and streaks as you go. Change colors and let the dye colors blend together. Leave extra space around each of the cardboard shapes as the colors will run slightly.
5. While the dye is still wet on your garment, make spatters with the Purple Spatter Paint. Remove the cardboard shapes and add some purple spatters to the white areas, too.
6. While the garment is still damp, add the lines of Bronze Iridescent. Draw various abstract shapes directly from the applicator. The paint will absorb slightly into the damp fabric and give a less dimensional line than on dry fabric. This will result in an interesting iridescent pattern. Let garment dry flat and repeat design on reverse side.
7. Allow paints to dry thoroughly (48 hours) and wash garment to soften fabric before wearing. Wash separately in warm water adding fabric softener to final rinse.

Southwest Fashions

SOUTHWEST FLAIR
Lael Furgeson, designer

The look of the Southwest is captured in this wonderful outfit that started as a simple white Tee shirt and skirt. The Indian yoke design is perfect in shades of turquoise, gold and bronze. Gold studs set in dimensional paint completes the look.

Materials Used

White cotton or cotton blend Tee shirt (long or short sleeves) and matching skirt
Turquoise Slick Paint
Bronze Iridescent Paint
Copper Iridescent Paint
Gold Glitter
Liquid Gold Iridescent Paint
Gold TULIP dye
Gold flat back stones (4 large & 8 medium)
Plastic spray bottle
Sponge

The bracelets and earrings shown are wooden. Start decorating with a base of Gold or Bronze Metallic Paint. Let dry and sponge paint Turquoise Slick Paint and a touch of Gold Glitter Paint to achieve an antique finish. Let the base coat dry and add the dimensional designs of paint right from the tube.

Before painting wash and dry new garments. The first step is to create the subtle background color. Pour the Gold TULIP dye into a plastic spray bottle and add 2½ times the same amount of water. Shake to mix. Line your entire garment with plastic and protect your work area as well. Hold the spray bottle about 30″ above the garment and spray to create the soft background color. Let dry, turn garment over and spray again to match reverse side. Let dry flat.

Trace and cut out the geometric shapes. Use graph paper and cut several of each shape. This will make it easy for you to layout the pattern on your garment. Pin the pattern in place to make the yoke design as shown. Trace around each shape with a chalk pencil. Draw the lines, dots and other simple shapes that make up the geometric pattern.

Outline all the large geometric shapes with Turquoise Slick Paint. Make dimensional lines right from the applicator.

Attach the gold flat back stones with Gold Glitter Paint. Make a bead of paint about the same size and shape as the stone. Press the stone down in the wet paint. The paint should form a small ring around the stone.

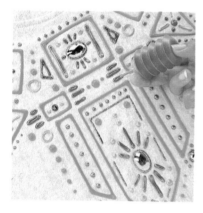

Add the dimensional lines, beads, circles and triangles to your design. Use the Liquid Gold, Bronze Iridescent, Gold Glitter and Turquoise Slick to complete the pattern as shown.

Let your design dry flat for 24 hours.

You will surely receive many compliments while wearing this attractive outfit. Add a suede belt, boots, and a hat and you'll have a great Southwest fashion! Use these same designs and painting techniques to decorate a denim jacket, vest or Western style shirt.

Fashions For Your Home

With a little imagination and basic painting techniques you can bring a whole new designer look to your home. It only takes a little time to create wonderful table settings, pillows, scatter rugs, lamp shades and more. The same sponge printing methods used to decorate garments can be used to decorate fabrics and items for your home. Choose paint colors that will coordinate with your color scheme, furniture, wallpaper, drapes. Remember that all TULIP paints can be blended together to create new shades should there be a specific color you want to match.

Materials Used
Cotton blend woven pillow and scatter rug
TULIP Iridescent Paints:
Sea Mist
Pink Pearl
Liquid Gold
Household sponges cut to shape
Plastic or paper plates

Pillow and Rug
The texture and weave of the pillow and rug help to create an interesting design. Notice how different each sponge design prints. No two prints are exactly alike. These unique differences enhance the designer quality of your hand painted fabrics.

Pillow
It's easiest to decorate a pillow cover that can be removed from the pillow and painted while flat. However, with a little patience you can achieve good results on stuffed pillows as well.

PAPER PRINTING
Edie Yerardi, designer

TULIP Paint colors shown:
Pink Pearl
Sea Mist
Liquid Gold
Ice Blue
Dusty Rose

Any simple line art design can be used to print with. You will be able to use each paper design 2 or 3 times. Make enough copies of each pattern to complete your project. Use permanent ink to make copies or use a copy machine. Don't use tracing paper for printing, use standard white copy machine paper. We recommend testing your designs on a paper towel before printing on fabrics. Cut out your designs, leaving a small edge around each.

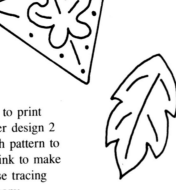

The first step on pillow shown was the sponged background. Cut a kitchen sponge about 2″ × 3″ and sponge paint the background color. Use a light application of paint. Sea Mist Iridescent was used as the background color on pillow shown.

Cut sponges to make the floral and butterfly shapes. Print the flowers randomly across the background with Pink Pearl. Add several Liquid Gold Butterfly designs.

Rug

The scatter rug was sponge painted using the same shapes and colors as pillow with the addition of the flower "burst" design. This was done using the small floral shape. Print the shape with Sea Mist, turn sponge direction and print a second impression on top of first. Practice a few times on a paper towel.

Placement and Napkin

The first step is to mask off the background shape on the placemat and napkin. Simple geometric shapes work great and are simple to create using a ruler and masking tape.

After masking off background shape, sponge paint inside the tape to cover area. Sea Mist was used for the background shown.

Remove tape. Print the large flower with Pink Pearl. See how the flower was partly over printed on background.

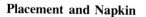

To complete the design, add dimensional beads of paint to center of flowers. Use Liquid Gold or Sea Mist right from the applicator tube. Let dry flat.

Paint a thin line of dimensional paint on paper design. Hold tip of tube directly on paper. Paint only one at a time as you have to print the design immediately after painting.

Turn paper over and place on fabric. Press lightly to print. The paint must be wet on the paper to transfer to fabric. Repeat printing until your project is complete.

This simple paper printing technique works great on tablecloths, placemats, napkins and pillow covers. However, you can certainly use this same method to design fashion garments, too!

Bow To Toe

BOW TO TOE
Victoria Wells, designer

Decorate and transform your kid's existing clothes with colorful fabric paints, beads and bows. This adorable fashion outfit can be painted on a shirt for any size girl.

Materials Used

Pink sweatsuit, cotton
or cotton blend
Grape TULIP Dye
Pink TULIP Dye
TULIP SLICK PAINT COLORS:
Lemon
Watermelon
Berry
Sea Mist Iridescent
Plum Candi Crystals
Wintergreen Candi Crystals
2 yards colorfast pink ribbon
Needle and thread
Plastic or paper plate
Three kitchen sponges
Scissors
Permanent marker
Chalk pencil

Before painting

Wash and dry new shirts and line with shirtboard or plastic. Remember to line the sleeves, too.

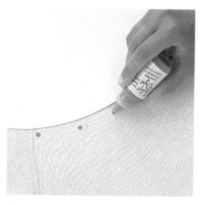

Cut a paper yoke pattern the appropriate size for your shirt. Use the Grape TULIP Dye to make dots around the yoke pattern.

When the sponge prints are dry, make the dimensional outlines, beads and squiggles with the pastel Slick paint colors.

Outline all the shapes and add the details to each as shown.

Using the Grape Dye directly from the applicator, draw a line connecting the dots. Make a scalloped line above and fill in as shown. Make a similar scalloped border at the neckband.

Outline the neckline and the top of large scalloped edge with little beads of Plum Candi Crystals Paint. Scatter the big dots of Wintergreen Candi Crystals in yoke area.

Add large beads of Lemon Slick to each of the scallop areas. Before you paint the row of Berry Slick beads along the bottom of the yoke, measure and mark the position for bows. Use chalk to mark 5 half inch spaces, at center and equal points from center to sleeves. Now make the row of Berry beads, leaving the spaces for bows. Let paint dry overnight.

Fill the yoke area with sponge printed designs. Trace the bow, tulip and heart designs on paper and cut out. Place the paper shapes on kitchen sponges and draw the shapes with a permanent marker. Cut out the shapes. Rinse with water squeeze out and blot to dry. Sponges should be slightly damp while printing. Use the Pink TULIP Dye to print and press sponge to coat. Make a few prints on a paper towel to check design. Now print the designs on yoke of shirt as shown.

Make 5 bows of 12″ pink ribbon. Sew to shirt in spaces along yoke. Add Plum Candi Crystal hearts to the center of each bow. Let dry flat.

Accessories complete the "bow to toe" fashion...Use these same supplies and techniques to make matching canvas shoes, socks and hair bows.

Beachwear

COLORFUL FISH COVER-UP
Edie Yerardi, designer

Paint this great little bathing suit cover-up perfect for the beach or pool. It's easy to do using the fish and shell patterns.

Materials Used

Man tailored cotton or cotton blend shirt

TULIP LITE™ SOFT PAINT COLORS:
Yellow
Gold
Orange
Magenta
Spring Green
Periwinkle
Green
Red
Fuscia

Wintergreen
Candi Crystals
Fine line permanent black pen
Assorted seashells
Small round brush

Make a splash at the beach or pool with these brightly painted canvas shoes and bag. Simply trace the fish and shell designs to cardboard. Cut out the shapes to use as templates and trace around the designs on canvas bag and shoes using a fine line permanent marker. Paint the designs with TULIP Denim Paints. This paint is opaque and will give bright, one coat coverage. Add the dimensional details and attach the wiggly eyes to fish with TULIP White Slick Paint.

40

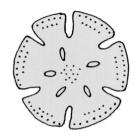

Before painting

Start with a white man tailored shirt, cotton or cotton blend, that is pre-washed and ironed. Select the iron-on fish and shell designs. Cut out and arrange on your shirt. Follow directions for transfering designs to shirt. For a sharp black design, trace over the designs with a permanent fine line black pen.

Line your shirt before painting. Have fun painting your fish and seashells with lots of colorful Soft Paints. The details of the patterns will show through the semi-transparent colors. Use a soft, small round brush. Clean brush with water and dry when changing colors.

Attach seashells to collar using Wintergreen Candi Crystals. Make a puddle of paint the size and shape of shell. Press the shell into wet paint to set. Let dry flat 24 hours.

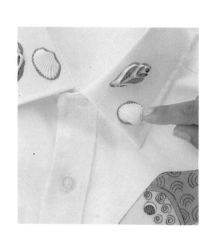

Beachwear 2

ABSTRACT ROSE DESIGN
Lael Furgeson, designer

Materials Used
Pink TULIP Dye
Aqua TULIP Dye
Lemon TULIP Dye
Neon Pink Candi Crystals
Spearmint Candi Crystals
Plastic Spray Bottle
Oversize Tee Shirt, Shorts Set, or
Tee Shirt Dress
(Cotton or Cotton Blend)

Before painting
Line garment with plastic covered shirtboard. Fill plastic spray bottle with water and spray a fine mist of water on garment. Spray areas where you will be painting and let the water absorb for 5 minutes. Lightly spray a second time and wait 5 minutes before painting.

Painting
The first color to be applied is Pink Dye. Shake the bottle before using. To make the circular outlines of roses, start at the top left of your garment. Hold the applicator about 12″ above fabric and squirt dots of the pink dye in a circular motion. Continue working inward and ending in the center. One circular motion works best.

Repeat the pink swirl designs wherever you would like a rose motif. Vary the size of the spiral designs from 3″ to 6″ in diameter. Remember to allow enough space between roses for leaf designs.

Next add Lemon Dye to roses while the Pink Dye is still wet. Squeeze dye directly on fabric making abstract yellow circles.

While fabric is still damp, draw two leaf designs on each flower using the Aqua Dye.

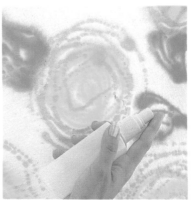

Dampen your fabric slightly as needed while you are working with the dye colors. Let the floral swirls and leaves absorb into fabric. You will see the lines soften and spread. When you are happy with the look, use a hairdryer to stop the dye from spreading.

All dyes must be dry before you go on to the next step.

Use Neon Pink Candi Crystals to make the dimensional design on each rose. Start at the center and run the tip of the applicator along fabric, squeezing gently as you go. Follow the diagram to create the abstract rose designs.

Use Spearmint Candi Crystals to outline the leaves and add the veins inside. Use the diagram as your guide.

Let all paints dry, keeping your garment flat so the paints won't run.

Decorate Your Denims

Edie Yerardi, designer

Denim jackets are a nice addition to any wardrobe, and creating a special, one of a kind jacket makes it even more fun to wear. It's best to paint on stone or acid washed denim.

Materials Used

Washed denim jacket
TULIP Metallic Paint colors:
Raspberry
Purple
Silver
Brilliant Rainbow Liquid Glitter
Black Slick Paint
Silver Glitter Paint
TULIP Denim Paint colors:
Neon Purple
Deep Pink
Green
Yellow/Green
Small, flat brush
Assorted silver studs

Before painting

Jackets should be washed. If it is a new denim, then it will require two or three washes. Denim contains a lot of sizing that needs to be washed out before painting. Do not use fabric softener before painting.

1. Use masking tape to protect area around pocket flaps. Paint the flaps with Silver Metallic. A small, flat brush works great. TULIP Metallic Paints give one coat coverage. Paint right over the button hole, you can cut it open when the paint is dry. Paint waistband and cuffs with Silver.

2. The flowers are painted with: Raspberry and Purple Metallics and Neon Purple and Deep Pink Denim Paints. Start with Raspberry Metallic and a small flat brush. Practice a few flowers on a paper towel. Dip your brush for each petal and make 5 or 6 simple brush strokes to make the petals. Don't worry about being perfect. Paint a scattering of Raspberry flowers on your jacket and continue with slightly smaller Purple Metallic flowers. Next add the Neon Purple and Deep Pink flowers in various sizes. Leave spaces between the flowers for leaves. Use Green and Yellow/Green Denim Paints to paint the leaves.

3. Next, paint the stripes on the collar. Use Raspberry, Neon Purple, Yellow/Green and Deep Pink.

4. Use Silver Glitter Paint to make the center of each flower. Start in the center and paint a dimensional swirl inside the cluster of petals. Paint similar glitter swirls on the yoke of your jacket. Add glitter lines between the stripes on the collar.

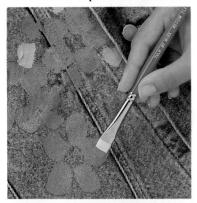

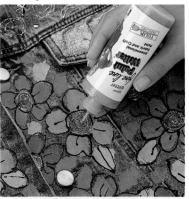

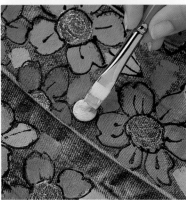

5. Use Black Slick to add the outlines to the flower centers, petals and leaves. Make black lines on collar stripes.

6. Paint the finishing touches on your jacket. Use the Silver Metallic to cover the buttons. Paint over the waistband, cuffs and pocket flaps with Brilliant Rainbow Liquid Glitter. This adds sparkle to the metallic bands.

7. We've added silver studs in a variety of shapes. These look great scattered among the Silver Glitter swirls on the yoke. Press the prongs through the denim and bend back with a metal spoon. When all the studs are in place, turn your jacket inside-out and brush a small amount of Silver Glitter to the backs of the bent prongs. This will seal the metal and help to secure the studs. It also helps to keep the prongs from snagging your clothing. Let dry flat.

Glitter & Glitz

Lael Furgeson, designer

It's hard to believe that this terrific fashion top started out as an inexpensive black sweatshirt! You can create this look in just a few easy to do steps, and very little time. The techniques used may be some of the easiest, but the results are exciting and fashionable!

Materials Used

Black sweatshirt or fashion top
(cotton or cotton blend)
TULIP Metallic Paint colors:
Turquoise
Raspberry
Green/Gold
Green/Blue
TULIP Iridescent colors:
Turquoise
Green/Gold
Mauve
TULIP Black Slick
TULIP Gold Glitter

TULIP by Marx
Paint Spreaders

24 flat back clear (crystal)
rhinestones

1. Wash and dry new garment and line with shirtboard or plastic before painting. Start painting the abstract streaks from neckband down. Using a plastic spoon, scoop a generous tablespoon of Turquoise Metallic Paint and place on the upper shoulder of your shirt. Use TULIP by Marx paint spreader (or stiff cardboard) to smear the paint down from neckline. You want an abstract stripe, so don't make it too perfect. Continue making the abstract stripes: Raspberry, Green/Gold, Green/Blue Raspberry, Green/Gold.

2. Use the Gold Glitter Paint and make various size swirls over all the metallic stripes. Paint Black Slick triangles here and there across your design. Set the rhinestones in puddles of wet Gold Glitter. See how they become part of the swirl designs.

3. Make teardrops in rows of three. Use the Iridescent Paints, Turquoise, Green/Gold and Mauve to make the dimensional teardrops. Practice on a paper towel; it's easy. Simply make a dimensional bead of paint and drag the applicator tip out from bead in one short stroke.

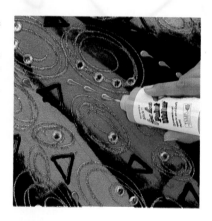

Let your fashion paints dry flat for 24 hours. Enjoy!

Directions for Iron on Designs

Before Ironing

Wash and dry new garments to remove sizing. Use cotton or cotton blend fabrics. The transfer ink will be lighter on all cotton fabric. Protect your ironing board cover with a clean, smooth cloth. Pre-heat your iron (5 minutes) to the appropriate fabric setting. Line thin garments with aluminum foil so the ink does not run through to back of garment. Cut out the design, leaving a border of paper around it. Remember to cut away any portions of the design that you do not want to transfer to your garment.

Place the transfer design in the desired location. You may find it easier to pin large designs in place. ***Place the pattern ink side down*** on the right side of your garment.

Ironing

DO NOT USE STEAM

We recommend that you test a small design on the underside hem of your garment to check the transfer ink.

Press the hot iron directly on transfer paper. To prevent the ink from blurring, do not slide the iron around on the transfer paper. Press one area at a time, lift iron and press the next area. Different fabric blends take various amounts of time for the design to transfer. Lift one corner to check the intensity of the ink before removing paper. Let the paper cool before removing.

The designs can be used more than once. The intensity of the ink will fade with each application. To obtain a darker print, place aluminum foil under the fabric.

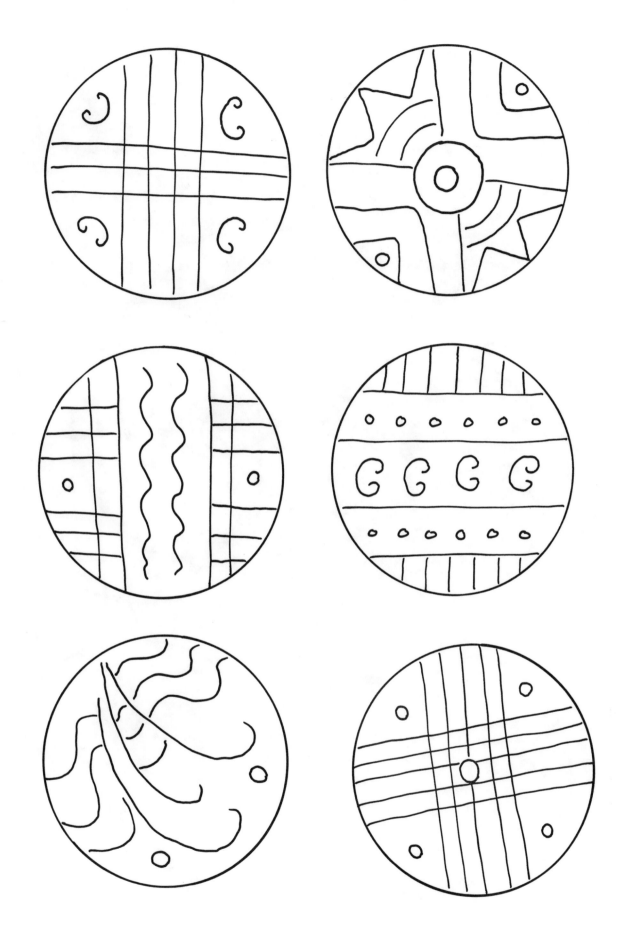

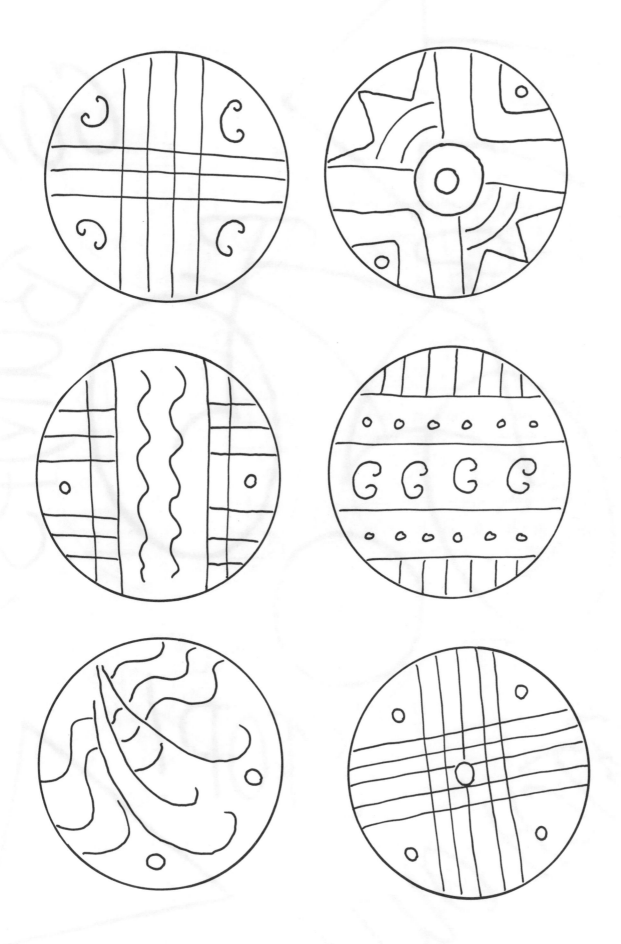

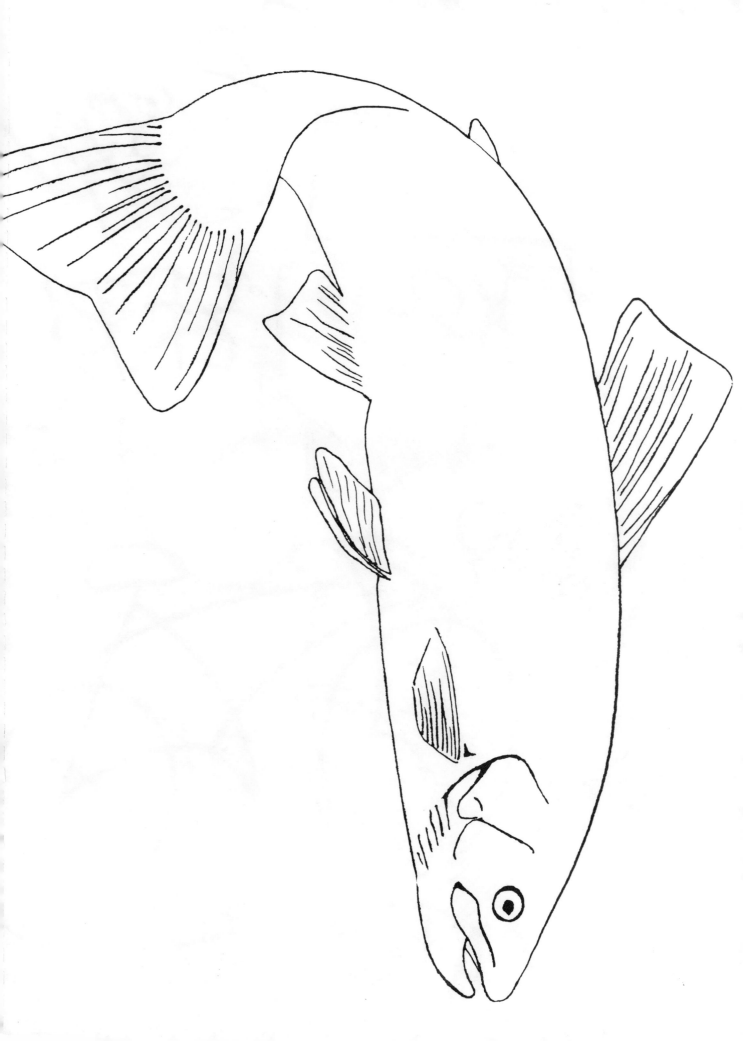

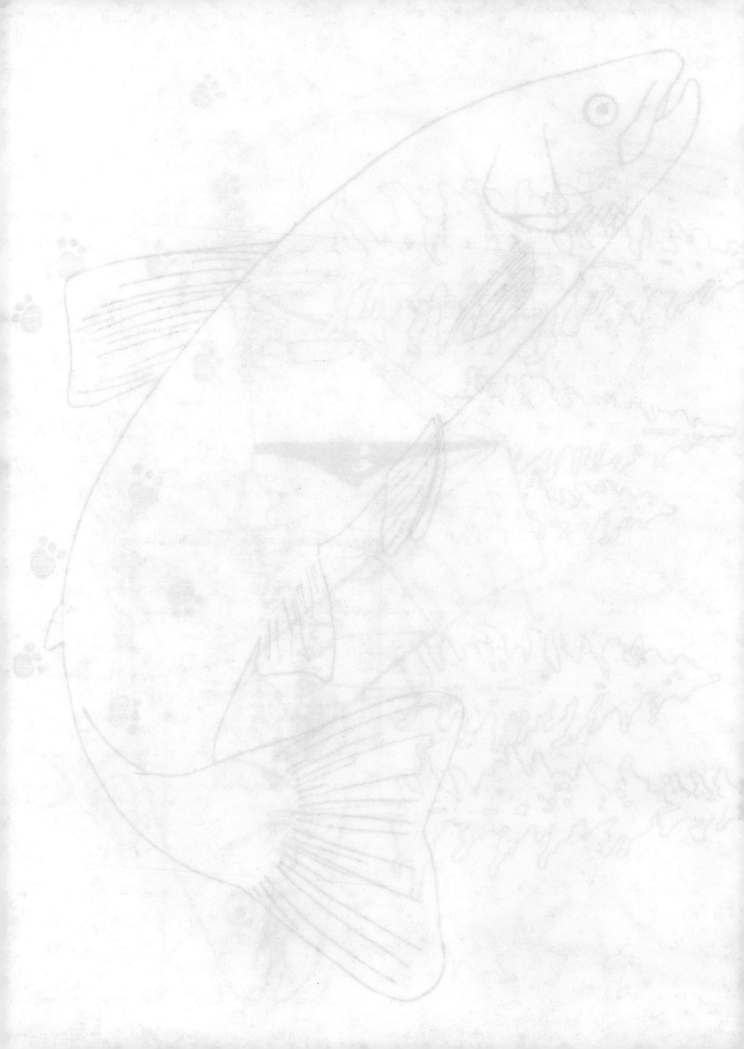

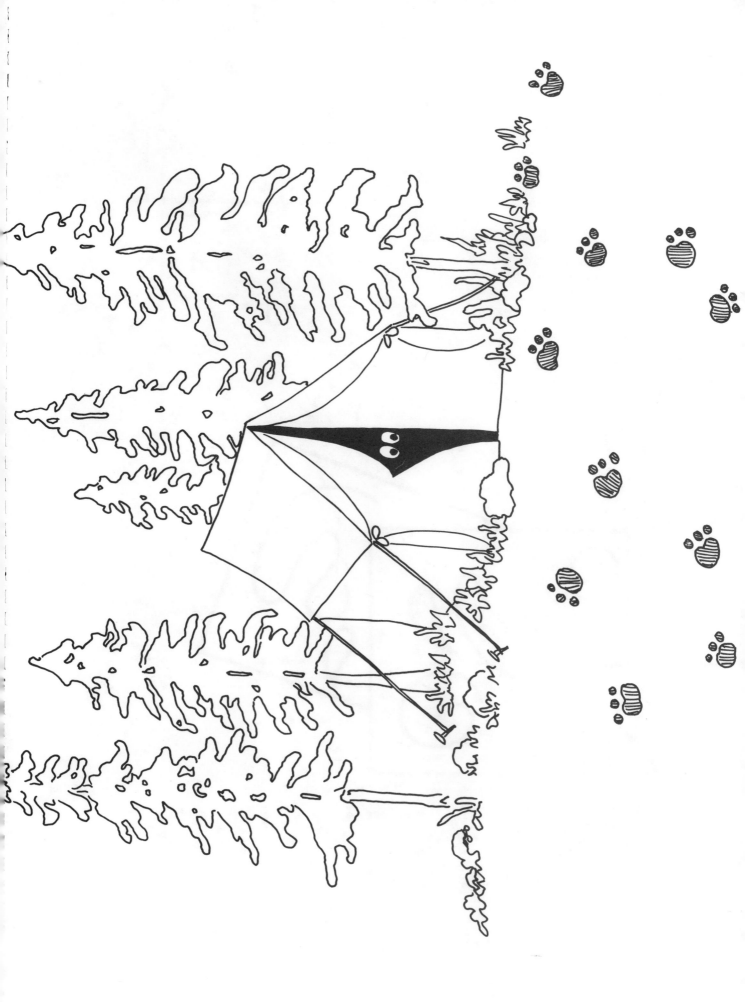

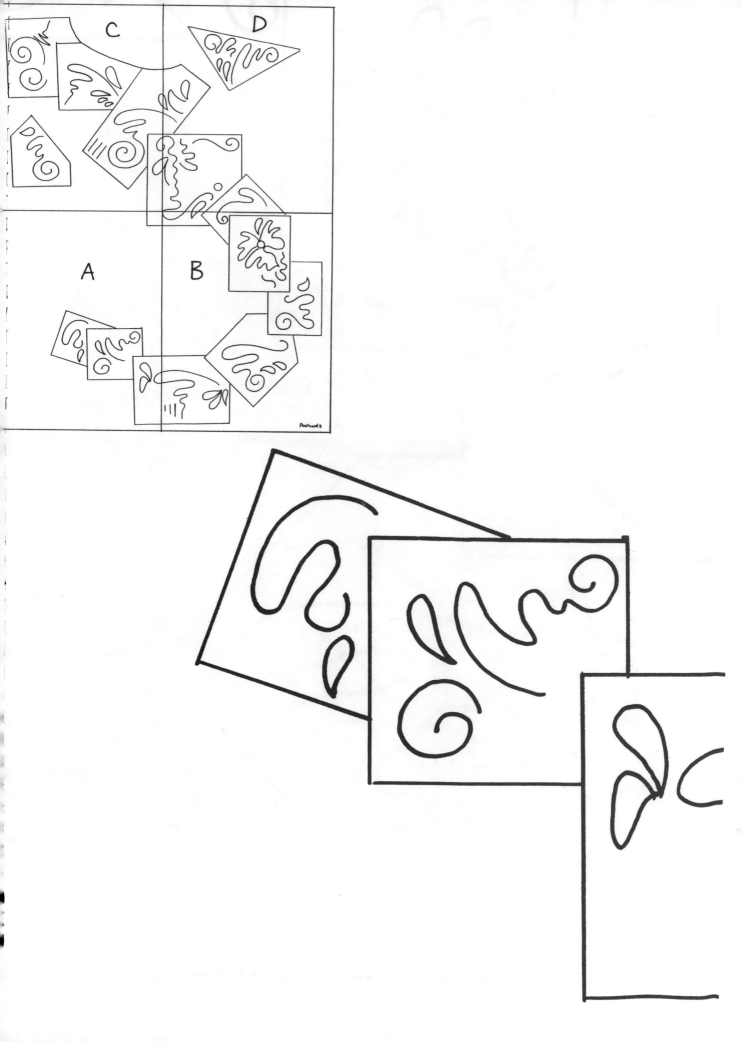

C

D

A

B

Postcards

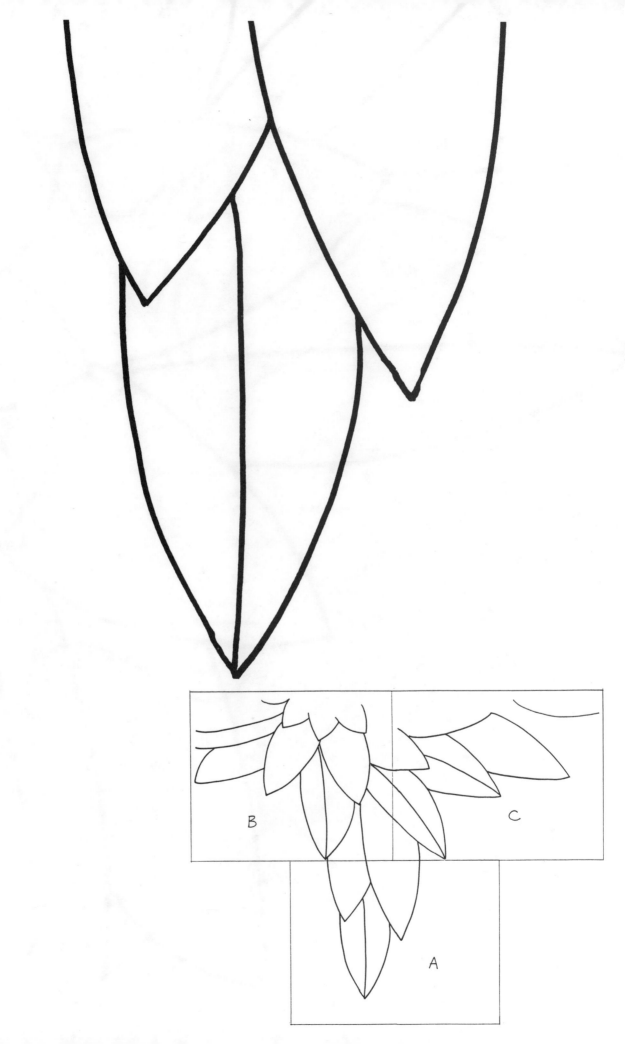

B

C

A

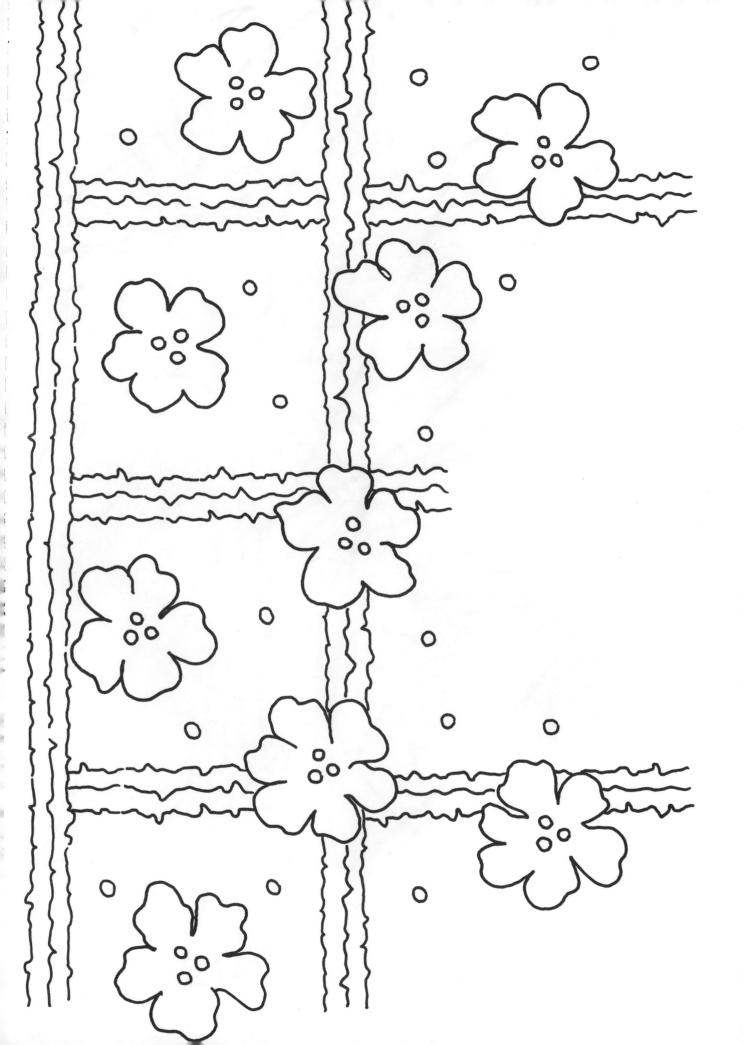

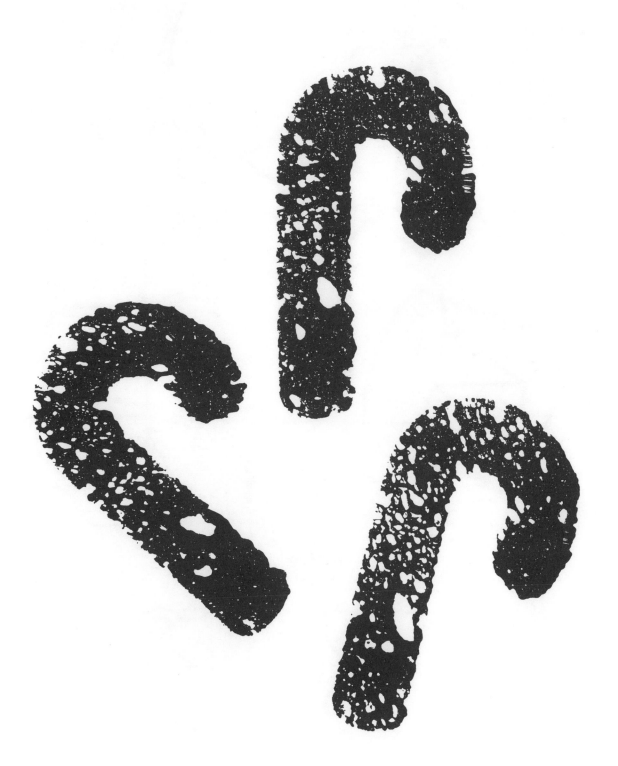

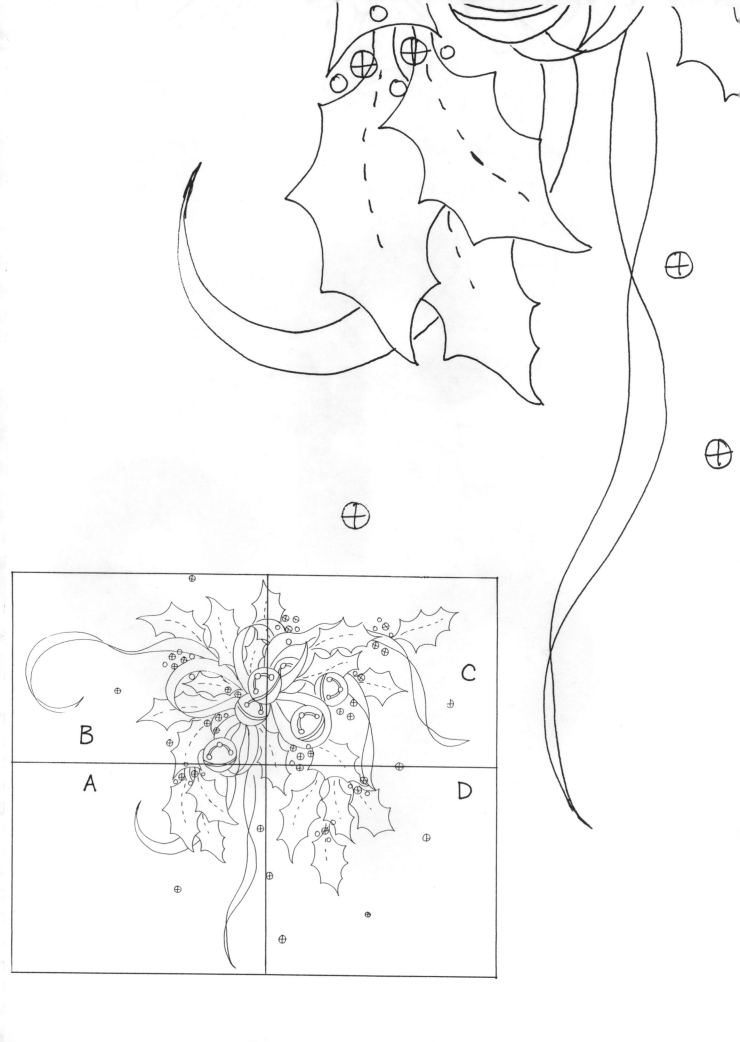

B

A

C

D

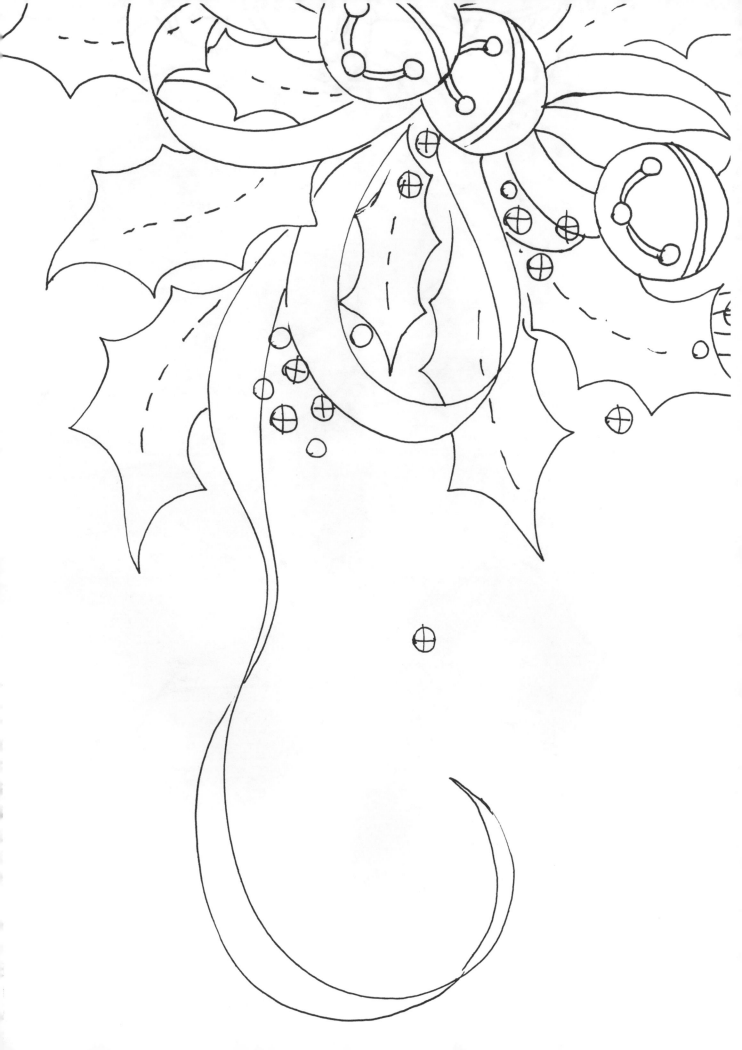

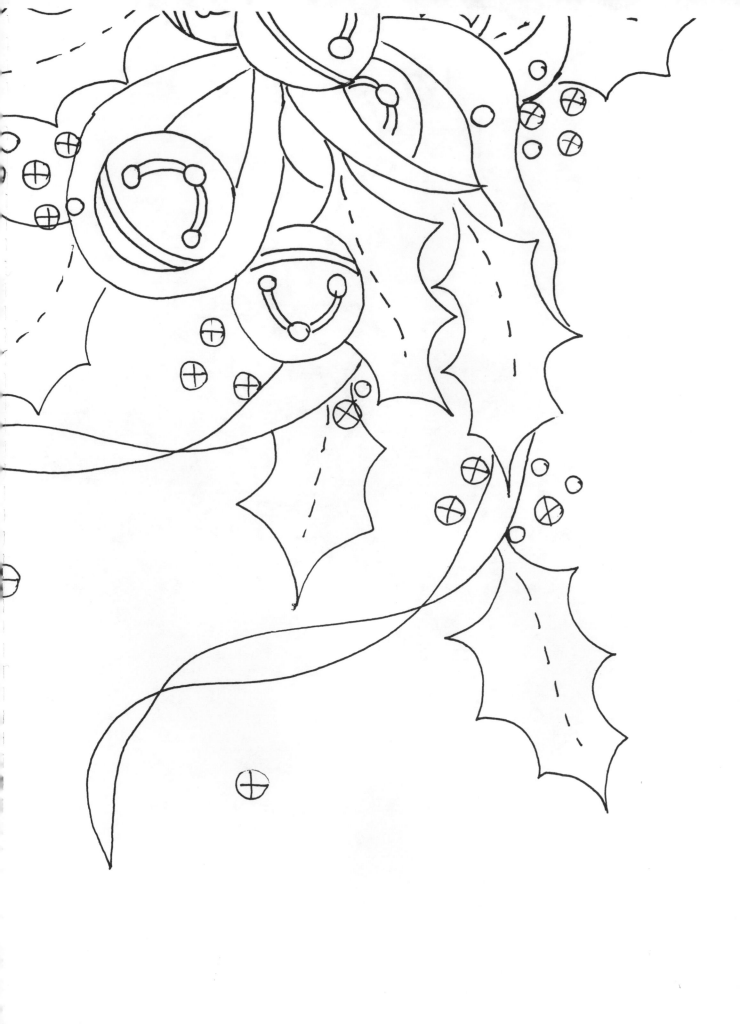

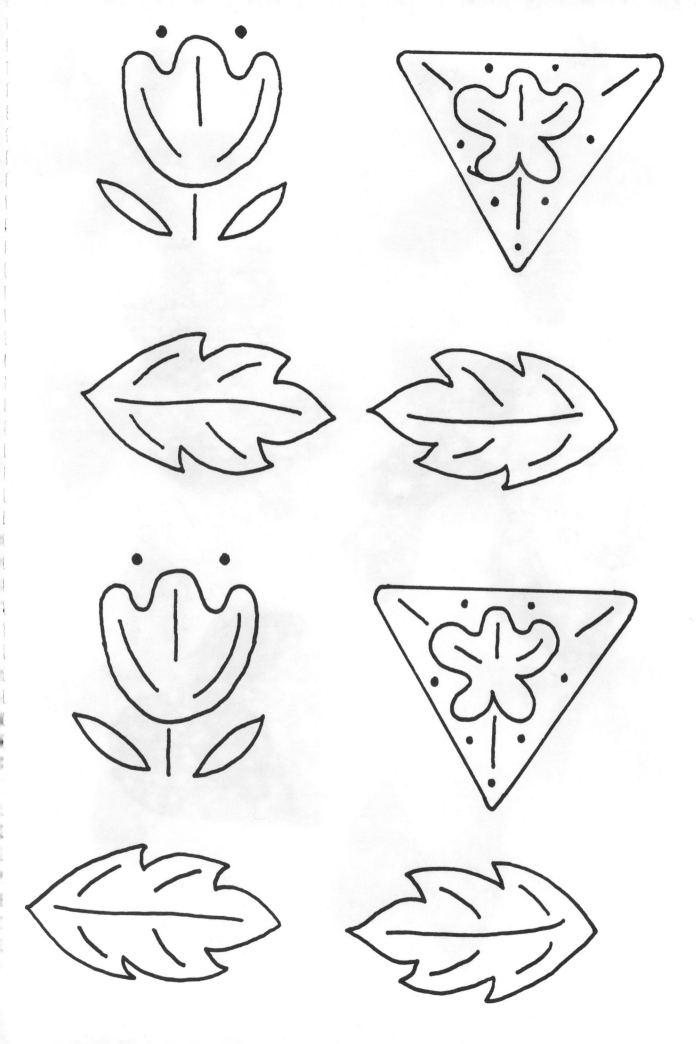

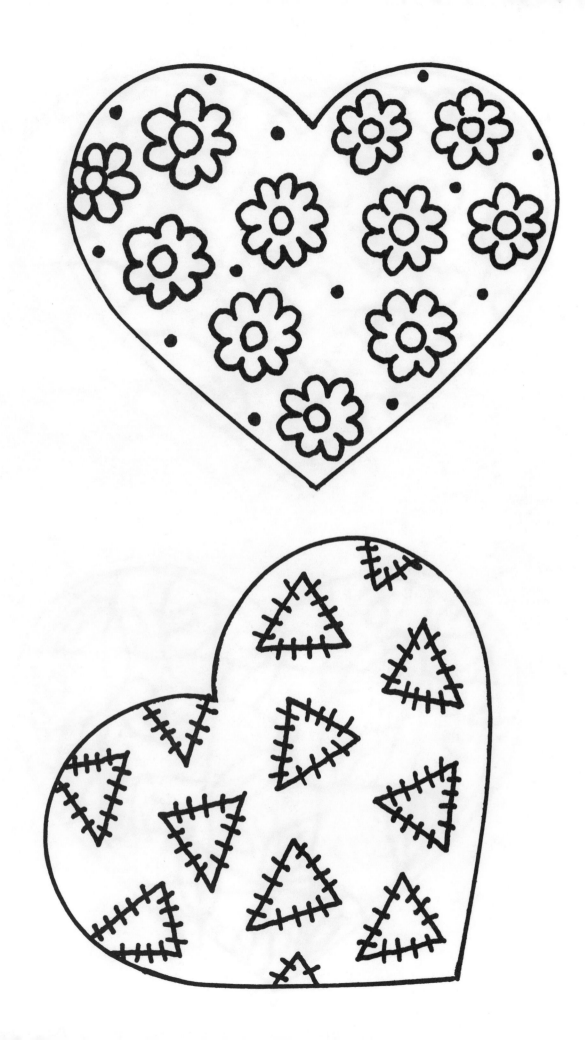

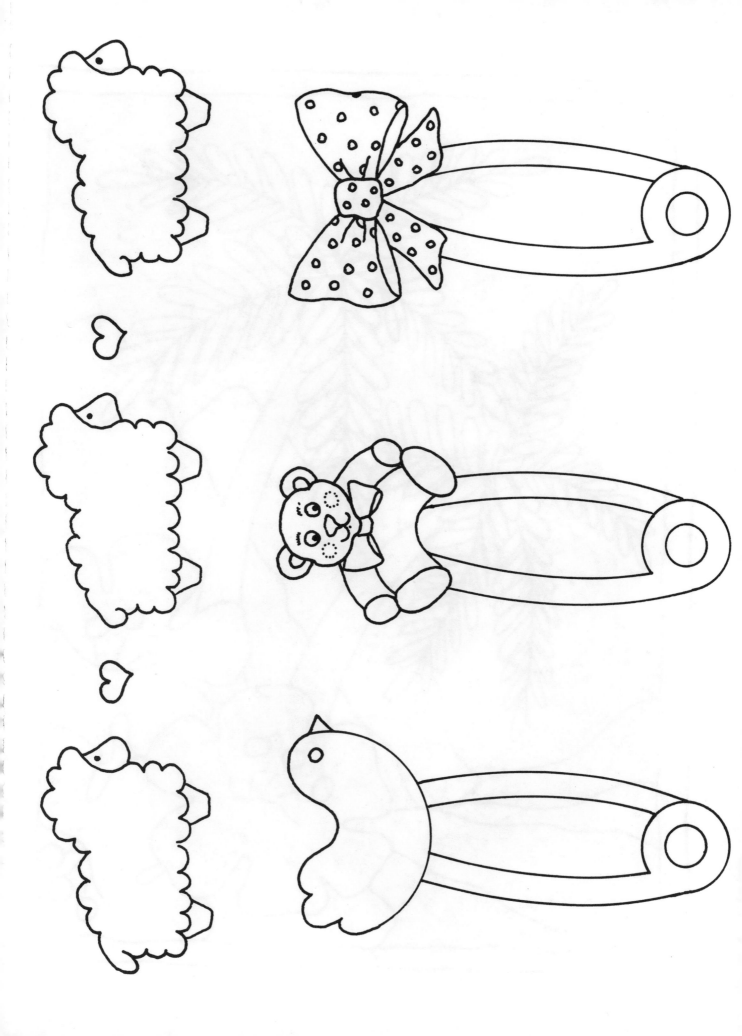